# Invisible Gifts
## Poems

## Maw Shein Win

MANIC D PRESS
SAN FRANCISCO

IN MEMORY OF MY SISTER

TAY TAY POE

DEDICATED TO SISTERS HERE AND NO LONGER HERE

Cover artwork: *Paint the World Out* (2017) by Mark Dutcher
Author photo by Annabelle Port

*Invisible Gifts: Poems* ©2018 Maw Shein Win. All rights reserved.
ISBN 978-1-945655-08-0. For information, please address Manic D Press,
PO Box 410804, San Francisco, California 94141     www.manicdpress.com
Printed in the USA

# Contents

## Blue Bells

## Pink Light

## Silvery Moth

## The Greenhouse

# Blue Bells

**Home**


The steps that lead to the front door are flecked with silver
dust and shimmer when the sun is low in the sky.

When the toilet flushes, it echoes four times.
Mismatched mattresses, Egyptian King frame.
A broken oven with a working stove.

The piles of paper, the piles of clothes, the piles of files.
Objects collected over years and years.
The slippers from Ikea so guests won't scuff the floor.
The houseplants that manage to live with little water.
The dust bunnies, the hairballs, the silk underwear.
The bent spoons, the dented pillows, the dental floss.
The boxes in the garage filled with old pictures,
letters, and record albums from the '70s.
Wrapped candies, Moroccan mask, tea bags,
plane tickets, hospital bills.

In the office closet, the ceiling is moldy, dark spots expanding,
too high to reach without a ladder.
The paint on the balcony wall peels off in shapes
of rabbits and deer.
A cigarette butt floating in a yellow flowerpot.

The neighbor crosses the street.
Why the recycled bins overflowing?
Why the flow of strangers leaving with office chairs
and toaster ovens?
Why the missing husband, the dent in the car?
Why the real estate agents in their well-fitted suits?
Why the cracked driveway? Why the overgrown juniper?

One fall, an old friend announced upon walking into
the living room for the first time.

*I agree the view is fantastic, but you're not supposed to live here.*

The hallway is a long corridor that leads to the front door.
The doorknob is diamond-shaped and needs to be jiggled
and turned to the left to be opened.

## The Wedding Party

The guests arrive
in twos and fours,
emerge from their
wagons and Mini-Coopers
shawl-clad and neck-tied.

They descend the
dry grassy hillside
like mountain goats
teetering upon
the rocks below.

The bridesmaids tight
in satin dresses,
sweating lightly.
The cousins and uncles
quaffing the merlot.

Flutes of champagne
and roasted garlic rounds
fly off the trays
and the bluegrass band is blazing.
Two old friends from college.

They make their way to the dance floor.
Long red dress swirls
around their legs as they arch back.
The wife of the man on
the floor leans forward.

Her eyes glazy and spent.
*His parents really wanted her*
*you know* she whispers *not me.*
Her feet hurt in those heels.
They make her want to smoke.

The children sit on wood
benches along the wall,
cutting out paper flames
scattering them on the floor.

The wedding guests spin on
their heels splashing the merlot
on neckties and shawls,
whispering bitter things.

*Such bitter things*
as the children stomp
on the flames
until their feet hurt.

## The Stalled Engine

She will drive for eleven hours.
Cathedral City to Berkeley.
A car in flames on the Grapevine.
She waits, unmoved.
An ambulance arrives.
The smoke rising in slow motion.
The camera pans out onto the landscape.
Cell phone battery almost dead.

She thinks of the opening scene.
The protagonist is in his car, stalled traffic.
Rome. Balding priest.
The anti-hero trapped, his head hitting the window.
Silent couples in their coupes. Silent.
Midnight. Her husband comes to the door.
*I have something to tell you.* A preface.
A line from a film. A disembodied statement.

*But first, how are you? I mean, I want to hear about your drive.*

It started with the broken oven
the phone call    the dance class
the nonverbal movement
*nonverbal    nonverbal*
the stalled engine

Close up of distress on the driver's face.
The film director rolls down the car window, wet forehead.
He floats up and out and over the traffic, the churches, the cars.
A parade of actors winds their way down the hill toward the sea.

## Stipulations

A sentence she thought she would never say:
*I am shopping for attorneys.*

The act of separation
The schedule of assets and debts
The declaration of disclosures
The accounts receivable and unsecured notes
The petitioner and respondent
The partnerships and other interests
The deferred compensation

The itemized as follows:

The stick bugs
The dried paint
The overgrown teeth
The silver linen
The milk trick
The bamboo shoes
The animal suit
The wilted oars

The falling from one mattress
to another one.

## The Hula Skirt

paper cut-out palm trees
encircle the pair on the stage
the dance has changed
master of ceremonies
in a white gown
parrot perched
on his shoulder
the dancers lurch forward
toward the blue spotlight
parrot pierces the cheek
of the minister
he starts to bleed

the dance is done

## Brutal

ruby birds and sound waves
a trail leads down mountainside
a physicist explains string theory

messages spelled out in dead coral
along highway that crosses the island
the names of the lost and the loved and the unloved

brown patches appear in the sky

follow the sea turtle
the monk seals
the newlyweds
the java sparrows
the hardened lava
the muscled bodies of the surfers
to the ocean floor

hear crashing against rocks and boulders
waves washing away brilliant and brutal flowers

**Cast Away**

there there
now here
where    a solitary pair

swims in separate circles
the water falls into
circular space

cast away
this year and another year
and another year before

on an island    the sand
and the land
where the pair

made a pact
to swim in separate
tides    trunks

truncation    a vacation
now here    not here

## Objects

A blue glass bowl of miniature oranges
three inches from arm's reach.

I eye objects in terms of distance now.
Reachable. Then not.

This morning I drop a plastic tub
of butter on the kitchen floor.

I try to reach it with my grabber, a temporary extension of my arm.
The lid slides off. The butter tips, and my cat starts to lick.

The objects in my life with more significance:
Wheelchair over umbrella.
Walker over work shoes.
Bed tray over sunglasses.

I measure distance from hand to knee to shin to heel.
I think of Burma, miles away. The grocery store, miles away.

My father's voice crackles through the phone, miles and miles away.
He: *You were born in Burma.* And then, *You're my niece, right?*

I push my body upwards from my wheelchair.
I know that above the ceiling are wood and plaster
and eventually sky and birds.

Objects, found and lost: my ex-husband's brown sandals,
loose feathers from a bird that my cat killed,
a large smooth seed given to me by a florist in Tokyo.

I look down at the floor trying to remember.

## The Dressing Stick

The dressing stick, a limb
on the edge of the green
and a twinkling star on the head
of a small bear, polydactyl paws,
matted skin, a seven-inch scar on the left hip.

She peeled the scar back
and underneath found a child
wearing a star hat and star shoes.
The hospital stood in the center of a large cornfield
and observers remarked at its beauty and precision.

They came bearing frankincense and painkillers.
They wore shields.
They could sew.
They came bearing pork and beef.
They held liquid in wires.

She waved the dressing stick
and the wires spelled words
through the window of the blue tent.

## The Wheelchair

The scar is a girl
and the wheelchair is a woman.
The crutch is butch.
The drugs are good.
The light is dry.
The air is paint.
The bed isn't there.
The nurse wears a cape
and the doctor is a boy.
The wheelchair is there.
The scar is at a loss.
The wheel catches light
off the reflection
of water in a bag.
The bag is on a pole.
The walker is a man in blue pants.
The scar cream isn't there.
The air is blue paint.
The light is a small girl
with her face in the pillow.
The crutch is a doctor
with a diamond on his forehead.
The diamond is a tunnel
with a one-way road.
The ambulance drives
towards the east.
The bed is dry paint
and the scar rejects the water.

The bag leaks a trickle of tiny blue diamonds.

## Things That Begin with S

*Sand*
Watery gray eye-lakes,
Sky gray upon blue, layer upon layer,
Jagged ridge, coconut palms frame vision,
A gesture here, skin against sand.
Blue swash over horizon.


*Signs*
Bluish, signage recognized, a face in the wave,
Eyelash recovered in the corner, a face,
Erased in the corner, blue truth turning,
Blue light, signs delivered,
Faint flash, blush lash.


*Sailboats*
There are things you have said.
I have heard these things.
Navy blue sailboats float along surface of water.
These sailboats can be words that sink.
And sometimes do not.

## Stray Cakes

silvery rivulets
on skin and pins
and nettles

snippets of sinking
singular she
shivers and slivers

stray cakes
unwashed glasses
she glances at maps of France

the rest of the body was warm
covered in many blankets
the cold wind came through the window

made her head cold
covered in many blankets
the rest of the body was warm

watery ferns
an optical ending
the optical beginning

## Softer Animals

It is raining. It is Thursday night.
There are 36 steps up to Anna's
apartment on the East Side.
A bed with softer animals.
A Doberman Pinscher walks into a 7-Eleven
and buys a carton of milk.
I notice these things.

Rain waters the buildings
and they grow and grow.
Makes thieves work harder.
Softens mountains.
Ruins sandwiches.
Some paintings make me cry.
I Like Crying.

*Gunsmoke* was a good show to cry to.
Also, *The Waltons* Christmas special.
Anna is reading about corpse
flowers in western Sumatra.
The towering plants bloom every ten years.
Anna tells me they thrive on flesh flies in rainforests.
I knew that already.

What I don't know is how lightning feels on the body,
or what makes a glowworm glow,
or why the neighbor keeps knocking his head against the wall.

## Mothers

This is what I remember: the sound of my head popping. Fleshy hands of the doctor on my back. Did I shudder at the slap of antiseptic air on my face or remain quiet and blank at the adulations of the cooing nurses in their white gowns? Or was I wrapped in cotton webbing, brown toes sticking out like little mice?

My parents met in medical school, Rangoon, Burma. Compelled by their parents to be doctors. Mother wrote poetry when she was young, read translated versions of Emily Dickinson in Burmese, daydreamed. Father sketched Marilyn Monroe in various seductive poses, scandalous to the family.

A green glass bowl of rice sliding to the floor, bits of glass mixed with rice and shrimp. My mother cuts herself as she kneels to pick up the glass. I sit looking down from my high chair, drooling. Her blood on the rice and shrimp.

This is what I don't remember: Ma was an opera singer from Bulgaria and wore a huge yet exquisite wart on her right cheek. She loved me madly and designated me favored daughter. She always remembered to pick up trinkets from foreign cities and leave them on my bed in the middle of the night.

Three weeks old. An infant placed in the care of a nurse who works at the hospital with my mother and father. Massachusetts. A place I don't remember, except from a photograph of when I was three. A blue little girl holding a balloon. Tricycle tipped over.

My new mother's name is Peggy. She is a nurse at Boston General. She feeds me Velveeta cheese sandwiches cut into triangles. I can hear a song about go-go boots coming from the den. I run in and see Janey her youngest daughter sitting on her lap. They are laughing and Peggy is kissing her on the cheek.

Ma has just returned from an international tour promoting her new recording of *Madame Butterfly*. My sister and I sit in front of the TV and watch as she is being interviewed by a reporter in a cream-colored jumpsuit. She smiles and waves to the crowd, resplendent in her Jackie O sunglasses. Blows kisses to the camera.

This is what I remember or rather this is what I don't remember.

## Dragonfly

The mountain I didn't climb.
Grilled cheese sandwiches fried in olive oil.
Loop of swallow.
Sun on my black hair as I walk uphill
out of breath, cursing.
Binoculars on the table.
Stuffed terrier in a basket, no eyes.
Empty organic red wine bottle
under a fit of stars.
Conversation with housemates about failed Mormons
and forgiveness and poets in Nicaragua.
Wooden box full of straw hats in corner.
Panic.

White butterfly circling a dead tomato plant on the balcony.
Two cardboard coasters that say *Berg-Brauerei-Zellerfeld.*
Money tree shifting, leaning to the left.
Cable car, crammed with tourists, climbing up peak.
Dry legs.
Desire to swim.
My mother administering anesthesia
to a patient in a hospital
somewhere in Apple Valley.
Ten-pointed crystal hanging on wire
sending fissures of light across my arms.
Dragonfly knocking against a window.

**Nine**


I was hypnotized by nine.
I met him in a back valley.
The cape he wore appealed.
I took his hand and followed him home.

Nine will never end.
An ally. We skateboard through the alley.
Our powder-blue capes flying
through the valley of nine.

We did it nine times.
Capes flung on the floor. Caps
hung on the door.
Naples, Nutbread, Noontide, Nightcaps.

Nevertheless. Nine is fine with us.
We swoop through space and time,
wild capes and caps, captivated.
Never ending valley of nine.

## Limes

Stranded in an airport bar, vodka with lime, missed flight.
Thoughts of my unwashed hair, knee pain,
my love at home reading a book.
That day. Feeling as if my body could levitate
from the office chair as I sat and marked essays.
Overly heated building.
Remnants of paper cathedrals
on the bookshelf. Tiny limes rolling off
a truck on the freeway.
Rolling suitcases down the aisles, hearts beating fast.
Looking at clocks and clerks, and finally the flat spaces
below through the window.
Jets' wings cut through trails of cloud.

As a child, I'd watch my father cut limes for his cocktails.
He would quickly squeeze a slice in the tall glass,
then toss the ends in the sink.
Steadying himself on the counter
with thin hands, dry and dark.

As a teenager, I'd drink with Lisa and Bob,
lime and lemon liqueurs swiped from our parents' cabinets.
Our drunkenness in the cold night
behind a church down the street.
Elvis Costello songs on the cassette player.

I would cry in my room when I came home after school.
I feared the future might not be what I imagined.

## You Will Be with Me in a Town Called Paradise

The sound of horns and bells, the sound
of round crowns and brown birds, blue bells.

You will be with me in a town called Paradise
with a slice of cake, cluster of cherries, champagne on ice.

The night we met, a New Year's Eve party, a talent
show. Someone pretends to be a stork, another pop of a cork.

Your clear eyes and warm head. I couldn't hear your eyes,
but I could see your voice. Is paradise this bed?

Two cotton blankets and a comforter on my side,
a light sheet on yours. Bluebells on the dresser.

You touch the cat's fur, orange beneath the chin,
she leaps off your chest. We rest for a while.

# PINK LIGHT

## Gold Barns Above Sea Level

                sea feathers
                sea fins
                sea whips

     how do we respond to touch?
     look around now

and even
they dream
underwater and above

                jupiter on red
                mars in blue smoke

silk stars
gold barns
follow the smoky trail to the end of the tunnel

     look around now
     a child in a bathrobe waving a flag
     look around    look around now

                see the timid dogs
                the brave cats
                with their stares up

## Time Machine

to a place
liquid and smoky

a boy on the sidewalk
long-lashed, laughing

humming birds
a disappearing act

we followed them
the heat in the room

the colors of bees
the blankets in trees,

the buzz in the well
fallen quiet now

hands and eyes
a yellow there and here

remote spring
such soft fires

they asked
on the shore we pose

with sea birds
oil slicked

enameled surfaces
questions

three drops of pale green
stay the night

***Art in America***

a smear of color and then as a girl in motion

    the discomfort induced by this cross-wired
carnal narcissism suggests a sort of discourse on
      the increasing denaturalization of nature and

  and the mechanization of creativity
    which mines the organic geometry
of genetic and cellular forms to create compositions

     that attempt to fit  the details
         of her own life
  into economically derived systems

        obscured by a thick dollop of lustrous
  pale-pink oil paint
    cryptic narratives

       map out the descent
    from rural grace into suburban angst
         *an obsessive quest for order*

notice the vicissitudes
  of personal existence
        travel endlessly in search
          of the sublime
   realize the artifice
     of your constructions

## Sparrow

There is a myth
that should the ruby-throated sparrow
land at your bare feet
while the sound
of a thousand crickets
fills the air,
a green-eyed mongrel
will come down from the hills
and eat all the baby boys.

*Look into my yellow eyes with love.*

## Pixie

Mother called her pixie.
The day she was born.
She said what a little pixie.
We'll call her pixie, and we'll dress her in green.
So that was her entry into this blood-red coal-black world.
Her infant dreams were filled with emerald ghosts
and terraced rice paddies.
Mother had a wooden cage made for her
which she lived in until the age of six.
By the age of eight, she had perfected
the Balinese Monkey Chant.
The neighbors clapped.
By the age of ten, her diet consisted entirely
of cilantro, alfalfa, and collard greens.

She felt nothing.
*pain   joy   lust   anger*

Why she was let out of her cage she'll never know.

## Beehives of Joy and Bliss

i.
while the goldfish swim in ovals
the finches nest nearby
so we continue

they hear the buzzing inside
she leaves the nest
we sleep in a warm cove

emerald visions
watery flights
beehives of bliss and joy

ii.
soft signals
light landings
such colors of seduction

a pause
then a thought
*why fly over the ocean at night?*

bright wings
colony of bees
buzzing of joy, buzzing of bliss

iii.
now an image
flickers through
the airwaves
*she came from the sky, right?*

the coral girl flies above
we see her sometimes
with her rose wings

the emerald nests
the restless finches
the nectar seekers

**The Unexpected Visit**
*Visita Inesperada*
(a painting by Remedios Varo, 1958)


i.
shades of bone and shale
a mummified bobcat

a woman covered with hair
waits at the table

two place settings
without bread or fruit

the blotted windows
or an arm through the drapes

a still death tableaux
of heavenly radiation


ii.
pay attention:
these trees are winter trees
this bobcat is dead
those shadows are invisible
this hand is held
the woman is waiting
these plates are empty
the visitor is unexpected

iii.
should a visitor come:
how would he arrive
through the shuttered window
in the blue-black of night?
through the octagonal
brick-layered hole in the floor?

will he arrive alone?
will he come with a cat?

or will he emerge from the trees
in a blister of stars?

## Dust and Smoke

He doesn't know I'm in the den. I am 12. I face his back. He sits in the chair. He smokes Kent 100's. He drinks. His rack of top twenty singles on the wall. He has headphones on. I smell the smoke. It hurts my eyes. I am barefoot. This is his room. The brown vinyl loveseat. The records on the shelf: Joni, Bob, Carly. My hair is short. I have bangs. The blinds are closed. The light coming through. Trail of smoke is a fairy wing.

Her father alone. In a studio. A door to a hut. Some white dust from the street. The white dust comes through the openings in the walls. He waits for the phone to ring. Dust on the photo of her sisters, her brother. Dust on his white hair. His belly protrudes but his arms are sticks. Hershey's chocolate bars from Sav-On in his fridge. Chicken curry with potatoes in plastic container. Dust on the table. Phone without sound. The street with the voices. Heads that don't look up.

## The General

i.

someone pushing a table across the floor: crumbling teeth
the mouth: tiny boy in the dollhouse
he sits at the front of the table: roasted chicken on his plate
basket of lilies on the floor: pincushion beside the bed


ii.

she glides past him while he sleeps
cloud arms move upward
she is the brilliant innkeeper
he dreams of a pincushion


iii.

look through the keyhole: the star-blood flowers
heat outside the gates: soldiers and monks
he sleeps with his mouth open: no sheets
she pricks him with a needle: red glass

## Blindfolds

the autocrats lost
in the wilderness wandering
the forest of delusion
or the reproving slap
of father, sir, boss boss

and the instability
of blindfolds that shield
necklaces of chains and nails
for soldiers
and boys

two thousand years
of longing    stupefied    tantrum
the oxhearts and oxlips
or the blackness of cherries
that burn through the snow

## The Contract

I am a teacher. They are civil engineers.
We study the rules of grammar.
I write on the whiteboard. Sentences in active and passive.
*Either an indirect object or a direct object may become*
*the subject of a passive sentence.*
He walks in late. He wears a parka.
He avoids my eyes.
The students look down.

We assume there are rules that both parties must follow.
A written or unwritten contract. He is anger and rage.
We can hear Pearl at her keyboard. A nine to five contract.
Two weeks off the first year. Three the second.
A health insurance plan through Kaiser. A high deductible.

We are nerves and muscles and vessels of blood.
We are socially acceptable behaviors.
We are brown blazers with lint on them
and failed attempts at connection.
Phrases and clauses and summary notes of longing and grief.
Memos to parents who are aging.
An email to the son lost and wandering through Georgia.
A text to the neighbor who undresses in front of the window.

We signed contracts. There are expectations.
*In the passive, the object of an active verb becomes*
*the subject of the passive verb.*
He brings his fist to the table. We have forgotten the contract.
He has not read the rules.

### I hate programming without free will

The baby wields a pocketknife.

The stewardess has a vengeance.

A chamber is a melted orange cone.

Greatness is tremendous.

Thunder is the underside of a walrus.

A chant is a velveteen dress.

The tourist is a red bloom under a carcass.

Manila folders are blessed with fragrant oils.

The power tools are powder blue.

Crack is a side dish.

Gold is a platter of overripe bananas.

A nightshade is categorical.

Truth is unforgivable.

A chicken is a standing target.

I love a scratching face.

I hate the twitter bleed.

---

"i hate programming without free will" is a line from the poem "after 'the lie of art' " by ko ko thett, from his book *Burden of Being Burmese*. "after the lie of art" is after "The Lie of Art," a poem by Charles Bernstein.

## Patrol

They carefully ladle the stew into blue bowls.
Bits of beef, slivers of pearl onion, mushroom.
A hard loaf of bread.
The guard patrols at the border sipping from a flask, shivering.

They remember that winter.
The wisteria asleep.
That violet hanging.
The warm body there, the lattice, the lantern, swinging, swinging.

## The Misfortunes of Guan Yin

i.
an oyster, still, in brackish waters
sound of fallen blankets, *di sotto in su*
three-chambered heart pumps transparent blood

the misfortunes of Guan Yin
her eleven heads and thousand arms
*eat up the master*

the daughter captive in the enclosed porch
father hides in the bushes
a scar on the girl's arm from a willing branch

ii.
calcified valves shelter fleshy matter
bony tongues and coffinfish encircle
the sea stars and spat

strangers and pilgrims offer snapdragons
and chocolate coins wrapped in gold paper
the mangrove roots have lost control

the sound of watermen scraping
the sound of beating cilia
holding   containing   opening   closing

iii.
nacre covers grit: mother-of-pearl
the evolution of an irritant
Russian blue, milk white

iv.
emerald green sash across her reedy frame
mottled skin across neck, shoulders
a girl dancing in the garden of her mind

## The Indexing of Sensation

Jean comes into the library and passes wildflowers into my hands.
*Put these in water, darling, and have a brilliant day.*
I push the cart down the carpeted aisle.
The repetition of movement is a meditation.

| | |
|---|---|
| *The Art of Benin*, Paula Ben-Amos | N 7397 N5C5 |
| *Anno's Counting Book*, Mitsumasa Anno | PZ 7A5875 |
| *The Forgotten Ones*, Milton Rogovin | TP 820.5 R64 |
| *The Balloon—A Bicentennial Exhibition* | TL 615 B34 |

Maps of countries that don't exist anymore.
The archiving of fantasies.
The referencing of systems.
The indexing of sensation.

## Are You in the Room with Me Now?

My therapist asked why I never cry.
I ask myself the same, closing my eyes.
A small sty in my vision.

As hard as I tried not to cry,
I was shy as a child. As I crossed the street
with mother, I hid behind her lab coat.

My throat taut and tight.
I thought I might cry.
The other night I lost my sight.

I could hear a couple on the crosswalk.
A man doing a handstand.
Two kids making plans.

Perhaps a chance to dance
in another place. I could cross the state
line. Cry at the sight of a shimmering lake.

My therapist asked:
*What are you thinking?*
*How does that make you feel?*
*Where did that come from*
*and are you in the room with me now?*

In Rio, there is a majestic cross on a cliff.
People live in pink paper shacks below.
I danced and I drank there.
I thought I might die there.
I crossed myself although I didn't believe.

You sweat silver tears.
You see through pink paper walls.
You think your body might be crying now.

# Silvery Moth

**Kick the Can**


That utopian moment
when the film begins
and the sound spins,
awash in honey and wine.

*Let's kick the can!*

Alive in eye of projection,
amber on aqua.
In Iceland they say *invincible.*
In Portugal they say *inevitable.*

Amplify echo of heart.
Modulate cadence of brain.
Cinematic monuments of desire.

A flash of eternity in the ecstasy grid

*Eye to eye, they solemnly convene to make the scene*

The version, the real one,
The empire,
Azusa, Covina, Fontana.

Dialing in the 909 in blind time,
The only one left of her and his kind,
The drive-by, the skip, and the skipper.

Mini-skirt mirage and dust bunnies,
Tassels and bonnets, trump card,
Wind winding round, sounding off board.

Out. Snap out of it. On the back of a flatbed.
A reappearing and disappearing
and tearing of the hair.

Clumps of sad lands and badlands
and ballads and frat beds.
*Welcome to Costco, I Love You.*

A burning and yearning, ballast and binge.
Stone. Dirt. Ice. White fire.
Blood dust. Stock lust. Lapdogs. Silicone and eyelets.

Teleprompters and dustbowls.
Orange groves and smokestacks.
Check the oil. Piles of soil. Spoil Him. Her. Me.

More. Tracking the score.
*It's keepin' track of the fact watching them watching back.*
*Come come now. How. Snap. Out. Of. It. Now.*

**Spine**

the iris is the bone
of the eye

eye blink

four times in the
face of a tornado

hyena cackles
spine twists
into question mark

flesh swung
around bone

strange
how the cause

is the cure
is the cause

## More Time to Do Nothing

It was an accident. She said it was and I know it was.
He was her rival and it happened in the heart of the backwoods.

On Sundays, she got up early in order to have more time.
More time to do nothing.

She had heard someone or perhaps it was some thing.
When she awoke that Sunday, her hair was in a knot.

A tangle of black hair, dense mass.
What happens in the woods when no one is looking?

Do you always act that way?
What do you mean?
Disappearing like that. As if you were picking marigolds
in a faraway meadow.
That's kooky, kitten.
You vanish sometimes. I try to understand why or why not.
That knotted up feeling inside, the woe-be-knots
and the would-be-gones.

Let's get back to her rival.
A slender animal, an are-you-kidding kind of fellow.
No knives allowed. Only sugar.

The last time we were in the woods together, you said, *I forgot
the sugar, but I remembered the hour.* Then I said, *Forget me, knot.*

Yes, there was an accident.
Do nothing, you said. Or do something.
Consider what your rival felt like that Sunday morning.

**Close Ups**

Two boys sit on a log in the middle of a valley. The trees surrounding them block out the sunlight and the boys have trouble seeing their hands in front of their faces. A woman appears from a cluster of trees. She holds a basket in one hand and a jug of water in the other. Her eyes are closed and she walks towards them as if she can see. She can, in fact, see through her eyelids. The boys are entranced by her silver hair and wonder what is in the basket. They stretch their hands out towards her.

## Ruins of a Glittering Palace

A painter in his studio
Glitter on the floor
Glitter on his hands
Hours turn into hours
A silver sphere hovers

*I want my fist inside you*

Layers upon layers
Cardboard, canvas, candlewax
Memorials to lost love and lovers

The hourglass
The crack pipe
The closed off cave
The empty pitcher
The medicine cabinet
The portals
The running teardrop
Braided rugs and waxed pansies
Feathers and spray paint cans
Paper chains that bind the wrists
The punctured sphere

The yellow brick road
The house at the top of the hill
Detritus of beautiful things

## Long Shot

She uncorks a bottle of Cabernet at 4:30 pm.
A slight buzzing in her ears. Pleasing.
A sliver of pain through her left thigh. Remote.
She thinks about her ex. He used to live here
and his shoes were over there.
The landlord sends a text. She doesn't respond.
She lifts the glass to her lips. Close up of her teeth.
Crooked on the top row. Straight on the bottom.

The sound of the fridge. Chilling.
Long shot of a woman as she slowly walks
to the radio and turns it on.

The voice of the radio announcer:
*Never mind the fog alert, ladies and gents.*
*A calf will be born in the morning.*
*Buy everything before you forget.*
*The song that you just heard was by.*
*More vision for all!*

## The Farm Without Name
(the home of Claude Cahun and Suzanne Malherbe)


she longs for her stepsister's hips
she counts the crumbs in her lover's house
she clutches at feathers with no regrets
she remains several women
she is a masked gymnast
she wipes off the sweat while no one looks
she is the heart of a woodpecker
she is a farm without name
*she longs for her stepsister's hips with half-closed eye and shuttered lens*

he picks the syllables up off the floor
he is a braided girl
he has never heard of the isle of jersey
he is a constructor and explorer of objects
he lives alone on the eighth floor
he has green eyes like fresh weeds
he is squandered and condemned
he is a farm without name
*he picks the syllables up off the floor and tosses them into the air again*

it slides to the ground
it fills empty jars
it grabs at linen bolts
it is Paris in the winter
it is constant as a cat
it is the mania of the exception
it is the public gaze
it is a farm without name
*it slides to the ground with its palms face up*

**Sometimes We Find Our Eyes**

1. A loosened sash

2. Singed flashes

3. Porcelain spoon

4. Blurred hedge

5. Flamingos in light

6. Stony coral

7. Blaze of glass

8. Violent poppies

9. I try to dry my hands in the fire

10. Sometimes we find our eyes

## Falling

It's been a long time since I've felt this way.
Well, not really.
I fell this away a lot.
Four months. No, three years.
Yes, six days.
There are a lot of things a person can fall over.
Logs, crates, puppy dogs, sleeping bodies.

What do they say about falling?
Help me to remember.
Something about livestock. No, ribbons.
All I can say is that I fell this way a lot.
If it was three minutes or eight years, I can't remember.
If it was the baby carriage or the chandeliers, I can't remember.
All I know is that I fell. And it felt it felt it felt it felt.

## Polychromatic Scenes

complementary fade outs. a smudge. on the lip.
depth of field. elicit a response. placement of hands.

      love's love living love love.
      their unwashed hair.

desaturation of periwinkle. copper tears from the eye.
liberated cage. keep away from machinery.

      silent film star gazes at silent film star.
      sweet spots (they said). hard to focus (they replied).

veins pulsing with...
lacking in...
gambling on...

      lanterns and rambutans. softbox.
      photoshopped lovers. polychromatic scenes.

loss and love over and loss of love again.
buttery blue love. swashbuckles of loveliness.

      lone dome. foment. lament. a nation.
      what is left over and out. of love again.

**Under the Pyramids**


evidence:
the broken window
the yanked open drawers
the knocked-over shrine

missing:
the poems
the film footage
the documents

the night  the trees
absorb the evidence
slap of the kitchen door
the screech of tires

somewhere:
the lost stories
in the back
of a silver truck

**Film #3**

He is a self-proclaimed healer from Holland.
He believes that people who are ill can be cured by
submerging their bodies in ice-cold water.
Men leap off cliffs into ice lakes in the winter.
Men sit naked in the forest up to their shoulders in snow.
The first thing he says to her: *You radiate pure love energy.*
And then: *You are unaware of your power over those around you.*
He finishes his beer and pops open another one with his teeth.
Close up of an ice cube slowly melting on her tongue.

**Collective Dreams**

i.
The ranch hand sitting on the horse
looking bored as a rabbit.
They fought at the wedding
yet the groom didn't notice.

ii.
The sun shot a glance at a
satellite circling the city.
A breathing and impervious endive.
An imploring and shifty senator.

iii.
The mice under the house
trapped in the steel wool.
Envision the ox eye daisies
tracing the hills.

iv.
The minutes last for minutes.
In Gokarna the Swedes gather.
In Pomona the Greeks lather.
And, in the end, they call it a day.

## Mine

cave below
tumors of coal
shimmering
a glint of silver
wild boys in the river
water to knees

slag heap over there
whether where
men go deeper
links lock dry oil
water hip high
brink of cave

snapped backs
black lung
slip down into
watery shaft and
soft-dark beams
breathing backwards

winking flame

## The Treachery of Images

The sun is a cymbal.
A cat is a bear.
An accordion is a frosted cupcake.

A gargoyle is a steering wheel.
The barber is a valley.
A tulip is a black-and-white film.

Architecture is a mustard sandwich.
A wild turkey is a forest.
The director is a fur sweater.

A mansion is a savage gown.
The guard is catnip.
A mink is a caveat.

The pipe is a magnolia tree.

The magnolia tree is a blanket.
The blanket is a flamingo.
The flamingo is a beach mat.
The beach mat is a soldier.
The soldier is a tangerine.
The tangerine is a villa.
The villa is a pony.
The pony is a peony growing
near an abandoned tool shed.

## Warning

if you encounter an artist at close range:
remain calm
pick up small children immediately
stand upright
maintain eye contact
back away slowly
collect branches
paint them white
observe the blue jay
skip lunch
drink wine
stay up late, very late
follow the breadcrumbs
call the cougars!
call the mountain lions!
document all sensations
be assertive—if approached,
move arms as if swimming
backwards in a lake
speak intermittently
and, above all,
do not run

## Questions for the Silvery Moth

Does beauty hurt?
> Only in the ribs.

Will the path lead to the briny ferns?
> Don't count your kitchens.
Antelope crawls its way along the freeway
> overheads and underdogs.

Do we love because we have to?
> Choose the one. No, the broken one.
> A basket of flesh roses. Bright blood. Kind cousins.

Does a cat feel?
> Insidious.

Why do we pain?
> Only the Buddha knows.

Who calls forth the longing?
> Sunny-side up.

When will the boat arrive?
> Push repeat.

What about your feathery ways?
> The ocean is silver because it reflects the sky.

# THE GREENHOUSE

## Invisible Gifts

Choose the dog collar.
Feathers dangling from the bell.
Mix beef bones and lemon peels.
Watch fat curl into fire.
Pick up cactus bloom. Blow out pink flame.

A box of ashes arrives at the door.
One paw print. One leather collar.
Missed repetitions:
Round tin tags clinking against each other at 5 am.
Dog dance. Leaping up towards invisible gifts.

Stroke his head on the hospital table.
Watch technician sink needle behind black paw.
One eye slowly rotating. Partial eclipse, blue
shadow passing over pupil.
The technician looks up.

Faint whistle in the waiting room.

## Flower Instructions

i.
Blanket streets with plum blossoms.
Rest body against warm concrete.
Find rose petals on sidewalk.
Glimmer of the memory garden.

ii.
Follow the trail of invisible bees.
Nectar guides for the lost ones.
Fling lasso into summer darkness.
Hear whistles and megaphone.

iii.
Hold body close to body.
Breathe in the greenhouse.
Wear wet glitter and silver hose.
Lick salt on skin.

iv.
Catch whispers in libraries.
Greet strangers with acorns and grapefruit.
Remember eyes, ghosts, smoke.
Watch brothers as they disappear.

v.
Imagine a new world.
Keep sisters close.

**shigo no sekai**
(the world after death)


What happened was this:
I was a rice farmer
who struggled to feed my family.
We were too poor to afford meat,
so we ate yellow cabbage,
turnip and rice.

One day as I was watering the fields
with my eldest son, I knelt down
and saw the body of a child,
no older than three years.
I felt my heart crack.
I had turned thirty-three that morning.

The child wore green knickers.
His face pale as rice powder
and his eyes open bright to the sky.
How did this child pass?

I took it upon myself to find out.
So I followed invisible footprints
towards the valley of *shigo no sekai,*
the world after death.

It is where I remain to this day.

## Another World

Summer brought flowers this fall.
We volunteered our skulls.
We slept on utopian benches.

Sometimes tourists
got caught in the crossfire.
The burning sensation.

We locked eyelids. We held hope.
Our bright torsos
wrapped in sapphire suits.

*Don't touch. Please do!*
Then spring shot wet bullets
into our electric skin.

## Durian

I am the lonely king.
Ruler of all, both sick and sweet.
I sit on my throne alone, woven
branch and leaf.

Cloak of spikes
and thorns prevents touch.
Hard husk, I trust
no one.

Should I crack open
upon fall or wall, a scent
so foul and rank. *Tremble
and crawl. Tremble and crawl.*

**Listen**

*I said rock what's a matter with you rock?*
        —Nina Simone, from "Sinnerman"

Spend summer
in makeshift tree.

Stand on all legs.
Listen to Nina

as the fires begin.

**The Worried Man**
(on a textile by Frances Butler, 1974)


A layer of months.
A slow moving moth.
Visions in the tower.
Picket line, bloom room.
Illusion. Infusion.
Factory dusk.
Elephant tusk.
Gas mask.
Optical signs.
Fines in the factory.
A butterfly fling.

The worried man:
How do we stay on the grid?
How do we pay the bills?
How do we find the ashcan?
Cloud in the eardrum.
Pillow book in the reverie garden.

## Hands

My father's hands, frail birds, shaking wings.

In Burmese, "win" means bright.

Hands that stitched skin together and brought back life.
Hands that held drinking glasses.
Hands that turned the pages of Hemingway novels.
Hands that prayed for liberation from earth.
Hands that reached for my mother's hand from a hospital bed.
Hand that waved through the bright hot air under a Joshua tree.

*goldfinch* and *waxwing*

*northern flicker*

## Lost Horse Valley

The horse is lost.

Needles from a Joshua tree. Cholla and ocotillo.

Quail, cadet gray.

Moonlit.

Wire-lettuce. Antlion wings.

He passes into the valley.

Left behind: three containers of Quaker Oats, bitter black tea
in a cup, empty suitcases tied together with twine. A dusty army
cap on the kitchen counter.

The youngest daughter clips his toenails as the monitor slows.

Another daughter flies over the valley.

## The Missing

i.

A river of damp green runs through the burnt orange valley.
The swimmers in the diamond-shaped lake at night.
The trees bust open, petals landing on cotton dresses.
The children have disappeared. Parents weep in empty homes.

ii.

A chalkboard. A basket of fresh berries. Lost signals.
The opera singer brings tears to their eyes.
The swimmers near the lake. Shivering.
A painting in the studio. Glittering.

iii.

The television doesn't work anymore. Nor does the oven.
The deer have gone the wrong direction.
*Turn around and head for the hills.*
The painter tracks green house paint on the blank canvas.
*The girls were in school to learn.* Their packed lunches in satchels.

iv.

Mother cuts the melon into sections
and puts them on chipped plates.
She calls out, *The fruit is ready. Come home now.*
Streaks of teal and vermillion. Layers upon layers.
The deer can't find their way back to the hills.

## Portrait of a Landscape

butter lupine and wild ginger, coyote brush and horsemint

we ascend the narrow trail trying not to step on the poison oak
winding its wicked red leaves along the way
past the sprawling eucalyptus

bobcat disappears up hill

v-shape of herons overhead, the movement of birds stills us

repetition of shapes

variations on the line

wind combs the lagoon, white streaks across green-blue patches

as kingfishers dive in for a feast

wild buckwheat and thimbleberries hide in the brush

the clouds observe us

**Skin of Oxygen**

table of lamps
bladder of needlessness
a cricket to green peas
grafting time onto sweet cheeks

stung garlic
the sound of Samantha
how flesh moves away from the bones
the cornstalks and the starlings

loveless amphetamine echoing
a breathless angina redoubling
a tooth in the field
a hand in the lake

abbreviate the thought!
incriminate the loved ones!
the potions posed
on the table like that

the semblance of birds
on the precipice of a cliff
buzzing of bees
heard from a clearing away

## Fish with Teeth

canal at the end
of the road     we walk towards

a year has passed
there is nothing to say

a body floats in the canal

green water, fish with teeth

*vines that grow from cellars of flesh*

the body is a plant
cut from its root, blue as a star

**Fortunes**

we enter the forest from villages,
cities, countries, continents
a canopy of trees circles us
bamboo, pine, cherry blossom

we consider our fates
among the animals that sleep here
leopard, dormouse, badger, raven
listen to bird song at dusk

we move alone together
swiftly, lightly
among flora of all shades
amber, saffron, fern

we hold thin strips of paper
threaded with twine
our blessings and longings
amidst the whistling bamboo

## Grapefruit

My flesh appealed
to you
that fall.
We fell
for each
other, flush
peach.

Though my taste
to your tongue
was bitter, you
remembered
my juice
and we rejoiced
in sweet fiction.

**5:47 p.m.**


*6:48 a.m.*
ginger-orange flocking
envelops wiry tentacles
pleated spheres
a flowering dilemma


*7:20 p.m.*
intuitive fountains
and the bells' allure
a flock of bird
cages in flight


*12:06 a.m.*
fervent seed pods hum
airspun foam ruminates
crescent feathers subside
starling in the echo lodge


*2:02 p.m.*
furred sound
partial recovery
a bottle-green beetle inches
its way across a limb

*11:10 p.m.*
metallic flake, russet yarns
slivers of ginger on the tongue
botany and reverie
the book of delight and other papers


*5:47 p.m.*
a girl laughing in the attic
a copperhead coiled in the brambles
a hedgehog sleeping in the grove
a slice of orange drops on the carpet

## Cellars and Bells

bells and cellars
and high-pitched
transmissions

nonchalant ambiance
holding at the station
blink tricks, whippets

pearly river
whorls, star whistles
syllables insist

linen space and blanket
-ed layers
*look at me now and here i am*

assuredly a shape
she stayed

## Almond Trees Uprooted

the stars light the face of the path—
green beetles traverse the grove.

stumps of almond trees, sleeping—
still breathing, limbs reaching.

benched stars, blanched dusk
sweet and bitter things bracing
for unknown terrains.

**Oars**
(elegy for sister)


glass rowboat
shadow falls across bright eye
finger glides

down

river, shaded by haze
slim arms, bright fingers
trail waters

long

gone, shades drawn
up, light bright against
the eye, arm trails

round

along river
below, the water
bright up

close

# Acknowledgments

This book is in memory of my sister Thwe Argy (Tay Tay Poe) who left this world in 2016. Much love to our family and extended family.

Many thanks to the editors of the following journals in which some of these poems have appeared, sometimes in slightly different versions: *Poetry International, Fanzine, Sparkle & Blink, Women's Voices for Change, Big Bridge, Cusp, Be Untexed, Zócalo Public Square, Artillery, 2River View, Artillery, Mekong Review, MARY, Maintenant, One (More) Glass, Aspasiology, Riverbabble, The Fabulist, Moria, Hyphen, vitriol, Monday Night, Babel Fruit, No Tell Motel, Ping Pong Literary Journal,* and *Up the Staircase Quarterly.*

Some poems in this book have appeared previously in *Score and Bone* (Nomadic Press), *Ruins of a Glittering Palace* (SPA/Commonwealth Press), and the anthology *Cross Strokes: Poetry between Los Angeles and San Francisco* (Otis Books/Seismicity Editions). Much gratitude to publisher J.K. Fowler and the rest of the Nomadic Press family.

My deepest gratitude to Manic D Press publisher, Jennifer Joseph, who believes in my work. I am indebted to Patti Blanco, Heather Bourbeau, and Laurie Kirkpatrick for their careful reading of my manuscript and invaluable feedback. And more gratitude to the members of my writing groups: Lea Aschkenas, Lynne Barnes, Chris Cook, Grant Faulkner, Kara Knafelc, Kathleen McClung, and Josh Wilson. Heartfelt thanks to poets and writers MK Chavez, Tongo Eisen-Martin, Jack Foley, Vanessa Hua, Genny Lim, Kim Shuck, and ko ko thett for their kind support. I am especially grateful for the arts and literary communities and spaces in the Bay Area, poets and writers, organizers and curators, editors and publishers, bookstores and art spaces for their continued commitment and hard work. Grateful acknowledgment to the following organizations for their support: Asian Art Museum of San Francisco, Headlands Center for the Arts, The Grotto, Squaw Valley Writers Conference, and the El Cerrito Arts Commission. This book could not have been written without the encouragement, support, and friendship of these lovely people: Youssef Alaoui, Jenny Bitner, Vince Blaskovich, Amanda Chaudhary, Yvonne Campbell, Sharon Coleman, Dayamudra Dennehy, Tim Donnelly, Penny Edwards, Thaisa Frank, Steve Gilmartin, Lael Gold, Michele Hament, Annice Jacoby, Evan Karp, Ingrid Keir, Patricia K. Kelly, Sarah Kobrinsky, Mari L'Esperance, Han Lynn, Vince Montague, Peggy Morrison, Kathleen Munnelly, Caitlin Myer, Annabelle and Ethan Port, Debra L. Pughe, Paul Quin, Paul Corman Roberts, David Ross, Pam Shen, Liz Sher, Martha Salomon, Susan Smyth, Christopher Statton, Chris Sterba, Judith Tannenbaum, Amos White, Audrey T. Williams, Megan Wilson, and Kenneth Wong. Much appreciation to my teaching colleagues. Thank you to my sister, Mithet. As always, thank you, Kelsey. I am forever grateful to my longtime best friends, Adrian de la Peña and Mark Dutcher, who have supported me with their love and creative inspiration over all these years. Finally, my deepest love and gratitude to my partner in time, Thomas Scandura.

And to everyone else, I thank you.